Practical Books
Pre-School

Planning
for Learning
through
Houses and homes

by Rachel Sparks Linfield Illustrated by Cathy Hughes

Contents

Published by Practical Pre-School Books, A Division of MA Education
St Jude's Church, Dulwich Road, Herne Hill, London, SE24 0PB Tel. 020 7738 5454
Reprinted 2012. Revised edition © MA Education Ltd 2008.
First edition © Step Forward Publishing Limited 2002.
www.practicalpreschoolbooks.com
Back cover image © iStockphoto.com/Diego Cervo

Planning for Learning through Houses and Homes ISBN: 978-1-90457-570-2

Whoo!!!

Making plans

Why plan?

The purpose of planning is to make sure that all children enjoy a broad and balanced curriculum. All planning should be useful. Plans are working documents that you spend time preparing, but which should later repay your efforts. Try to be concise. This will help you in finding information quickly when you need it.

Long-term plans

Preparing a long-term plan, which maps out the curriculum during a year or even two, will help you to ensure that you are providing a variety of activities and are meeting the statutory requirements of the *Statutory Framework for the Early Years Foundation Stage* (2007).

Your long-term plan need not be detailed. Divide the time period over which you are planning into fairly equal sections, such as half terms. Choose a topic for each section. Young children benefit from making links between the new ideas they encounter so as you select each topic, think about the time of year in which you plan to do it. A topic about minibeasts will not be very successful in November!

Although each topic will address all the learning areas, some could focus on a specific area. For example, a topic on Houses and Homes would lend itself well to activities relating to Personal, Social and Emotional Development, Creative Development and Knowledge and Understanding of the World. Another topic might encourage the

appreciation of stories. Try to make sure that you provide a variety of topics in your long-term plans, such as:

Autumn 1	Nursery rhymes
Autumn 2	Food/christmas
Spring 1	Houses and homes
Spring 2	Spring
Summer 1	Clothes
Summer 2	Minibeasts

Medium-term plans

Medium-term plans will outline the contents of a topic in a little more detail. One way to start this process is by brainstorming on a large piece of paper. Work with your team writing down all the activities you can think of which are relevant to the topic. As you do this it may become clear that some activities go well together. Think about dividing them into themes. The topic of Houses and Homes for example has themes such as 'My home', 'Decorating', 'Furniture and appliances', 'Taking care of homes', 'In the garden' and 'Home for sale'. At this stage it is helpful to make a chart. Write the theme ideas down the side of the chart and put a different area of learning at the top of each column. Now you can insert your brainstormed ideas and will quickly see where there are gaps. As you complete the chart take account of children's earlier experiences and provide opportunities for them to progress.

Refer back to the *Statutory Framework for the Early Years Foundation Stage* and check that you have addressed as many different aspects of it as you can. Once all your medium-term plans are complete make sure that there are no neglected areas.

Day-to-day plans

The plans you make for each day will outline aspects such as:

- resources needed;
- safety;
- the way in which you might introduce activities;
- key vocabulary;
- the organisation of adult help;

Making plans

- size of the group;
- timing;
- individual needs.

Identify the learning and ELGs that each activity is intended to promote. Make a note of any assessments or observations that you are likely to carry out. After using the plans make notes of activities that were particularly successful, or any changes you would make another time.

A final note

Planning should be seen as flexible. Not all groups meet every day, and not all children attend every day. Any part of the plan can be used independently, stretched over a longer period or condensed to meet the needs of any group. You will almost certainly adapt the activities as children respond to them in different ways and bring their own ideas, interests and enthusiasms. The important thing is to ensure that the children are provided with a varied and enjoyable curriculum that meets their individual developing needs.

Using the book

- Collect or prepare suggested resources as listed on page 21.
- Read the section which outlines links to the Early Learning Goals (pages 4-7) and explains the rationale for the topic of Houses and Homes.
- For each weekly theme two activities are described in detail as an example to help you in your planning and preparation. Key vocabulary, questions and learning opportunities are identified.
- The skills chart on page 23 will help you to see at a glance which aspects of children's development are being addressed as a focus each week.
- As children take part in the Houses and Homes topic activities, their learning will progress. 'Collecting evidence' on page 22 explains how you might monitor children's achievements.
- Find out on page 20 how the topic can be brought together in a grand finale involving parents, children and friends.
- There is additional material to support the working partnership of families and children in the form of

a 'Home links' page, and a photocopiable parent's page found at the back of the book.

It is important to appreciate that the ideas presented in this book will only be a part of your planning. Many activities that will be taking place as routine in your group may not be mentioned. For example, it is assumed that sand, dough, water, puzzles, floor toys and large scale apparatus are part of the Early Years Foundation Stage, as are the opportunities to develop ICT skills. Role-play areas, stories, rhymes and singing, and group discussion times are similarly assumed to be happening each week although they may not be a focus for described activities. Groups should also ensure that there is a balance of adult-led and child-initiated activities.

Using this book in Northern Ireland, Scotland and Wales

Although the curriculum guidelines in Northern Ireland, Scotland and Wales differ, the activities in this book are still appropriate for use throughout the United Kingdom. They are designed to promote the development of early skills and to represent good practice in the early years

Glossary

EYFS: Early Years Foundation Stage
ELG: Early Learning Goal

Using the 'Early Learning Goals'

Having chosen your topic and made your medium-term plans you can use the Statutory Framework for the Early Years Foundation Stage (2007) to highlight the key learning opportunities your activities will address. The Early Learning Goals are split into six areas: Personal, Social and Emotional Development; Communication, Language and Literacy; Problem Solving, Reasoning and Numeracy; Knowledge and Understanding of the World; Physical Development and Creative Development. Do not expect each of your topics to cover every goal but your long-term plans should allow for all of them to be addressed by the time a child enters Year 1.

The following section lists the Early Learning Goals in point form to show what children are expected to be able to do in each area of learning by the time they enter Year 1. These points will be used throughout this book to show how activities for a topic on Houses and Homes link to these expectations. For example, Personal, Social and Emotional Development point 7 is 'form good relationships with adults and peers'. Activities suggested which provide the opportunity for children to do this will have the reference PS7. This will enable you to see which parts of the Early Learning Goals are covered in a given week and plan for areas to be revisited and developed.

In addition, you can ensure that activities offer variety in the goals to be encountered. Often a similar activity may be carried out to achieve different learning objectives. For example, during this topic children use shapes to print patterns for wallpaper. Children will be developing areas of Problem Solving, Reasoning and Numeracy as they recognise shapes and talk about the patterns. They will be using creative skills as they choose colours and shapes to form the patterns. It is important, therefore, that activities have clearly defined objectives so that these may be emphasised during the activity and for recording purposes.

Personal, Social and Emotional Development (PS)

This area of learning covers important aspects of development that affect the way children learn, behave and relate to others.

By the end of the EYFS most children should:

PS1   Continue to be interested, excited and motivated to learn.

PS2   Be confident to try new activities, initiate ideas and speak in a familiar group.

PS3   Maintain attention, concentrate, and sit quietly when appropriate.

PS4   Respond to significant experiences, showing a range of feelings when appropriate.

PS5   Have a developing awareness of their own needs, views and feelings, and be sensitive to the needs, views and feelings of others.

PS6   Have a developing respect for their own cultures and beliefs and those of other people.

PS7   Form good relationships with peers and adults.

PS8   Work as part of a group or class taking turns and sharing fairly; understanding that there need to be agreed values and codes of behaviour for groups of people, including adults and children, to work harmoniously.

PS9   Understand what is right, what is wrong and why.

PS10   Consider the consequences of their words and actions for themselves and others.

PS11   Dress and undress independently and manage their own personal hygiene.

PS12   Select and use activities and resources independently.

PS13   Understand that people have different needs, views, cultures and beliefs that need to be treated with respect.

PS14   Understand that they can expect others to treat their needs, views, cultures and beliefs with respect.

The topic of Houses and Homes offers many opportunities for children's personal, social and emotional development. Time spent discussing features of homes and preferences for decorating will encourage children to speak in a group, to be interested and to consider consequences. By participating in circle times children will learn to take turns and to understand the need for agreed codes of behaviour. Many of the areas outlined above, though, will be covered on an almost incidental basis as children carry out the activities described in this book for the other areas of learning. During undirected free choice times they will be developing PS12, whilst any small group activity that involves working with an adult will help children to work towards PS7.

Communication, Language and Literacy (L)

By the end of the EYFS most children should:

L1   Interact with others, negotiating plans and activities and taking turns in conversation.

L2   Enjoy listening to and using spoken and written language, and readily turn to it in their play and learning.

L3   Sustain attentive listening, responding to what they have heard with relevant comments, questions or actions.

L4   Listen with enjoyment and respond to stories, songs and other music, rhymes and poems and make up their own stories, songs, rhymes and poems.

L5   Extend their vocabulary, exploring the meanings and sounds of new words.

L6   Speak clearly and audibly with confidence and control and show awareness of the listener.

L7   Use language to imagine and recreate roles and experiences .

L8   Use talk to organise, sequence and clarify thinking, ideas, feelings and events.

L9   Hear and say sounds in words in the order in which they occur.

L10   Link sounds to letters, naming and sounding the letters of the alphabet.

L11   Use their phonic knowledge to write simple regular words and make phonetically plausible attempts at more complex words.

L12   Explore and experiment with sounds, words and texts.

L13   Retell narratives in the correct sequence, drawing on language patterns of stories.

L14   Read a range of familiar and common words and simple sentences independently.

L15   Know that print carries meaning and, in English, is read from left to right and top to bottom.

L16   Show an understanding of the elements of stories, such as main character, sequence of events and openings and how information can be found in non-fiction texts to answer questions about where, who, why and how.

L17   Attempt writing for various purposes, using features of different forms such as lists, stories and instructions.

L18   Write their own names and other things such as labels and captions, and begin to form simple sentences, sometimes using punctuation.

L19   Use a pencil and hold it effectively to form recognisable letters, most of which are correctly formed.

There is a wide range of quality fiction books which feature homes and houses. A number of the activities suggested are based on well-known picture books and stories. They allow children to enjoy listening to the books and to respond in a variety of ways to what they hear, reinforcing and extending their vocabularies. Throughout the topic opportunities are described in which children are encouraged to use descriptive vocabulary and to see some of their ideas recorded in both pictures and words. Role-play areas are described that will allow children to use their imaginations as they work in a garden centre and a wallpaper shop, sell homes as an estate agent or simply enjoy housework and entertaining in the home corner.

Problem Solving, Reasoning and Numeracy (N)

By the end of the EYFS most children should:

N1   Say and use number names in order in familiar contexts.

N2   Count reliably up to ten everyday objects.

N3   Recognise numerals 1 to 9.

N4   use developing mathematical ideas and methods to solve practical problems.

N5   In practical activities and discussion, begin to use the vocabulary involved in adding and subtracting.

N6   Use language such as 'more' or 'less' to compare two numbers.

N7   Find one more or one less than a number from one to ten.

N8   Begin to relate addition to combining two groups of objects and subtraction to 'taking away'.

N9   Use language such as 'greater', 'smaller', heavier' or 'lighter' to compare quantities.

N10   Talk about, recognise and recreate simple patterns.

N11   Use language such as 'circle' or 'bigger' to describe the shape and size of solids and flat shapes.

N12   Use everyday words to describe position

The theme of Houses and Homes provides a meaningful context for mathematical activities. Children are given opportunities to explore shapes and size as they compare paintbrushes, print wallpaper, measure model houses and sort wallpaper shapes. The opportunity to count occurs as children collaborate to make a block graph of door colours, see how many coins foil houseboats can hold and participate in a number rhyme. Door numbers and a number line of houses encourage children to recognise and order numbers.

Knowledge and Understanding of the World (K)

By the end of the EYFS most children should:

K1   Investigate objects and materials by using all of their senses as appropriate.

K2   Find out about, and identify, some features of living things, objects and events they observe.

K3   Look closely at similarities, differences, patterns and change.

K4   Ask questions about why things happen and how things work.

K5   Build and construct with a wide range of objects, selecting appropriate resources and adapting their work where necessary.

K6   Select the tools and techniques they need to shape, assemble and join materials they are using.

K7   Find out about and identify the uses of everyday technology and use information and communication technology and programmable toys to support their learning.

K8   Find out about past and present events in their own lives, and in those of their families and other people they know observe.

K9   Find out about and identify features in the place they live and the natural world.

K10   Find out about their environment, and talk about those features they like and dislike.

K11   Begin to know about their own cultures and beliefs and those of other people.

The topic of Houses and Homes offers many opportunities for children to make observations, to ask questions and to compare. As they explore the best way to make waterproof 'For sale' signs and look at pictures of homes from around the world they are encouraged to notice details. Through making modelhomes children gain a greater understanding of the properties of materials and have the opportunity to explore ways to join materials. Through all the activities children are encouraged to talk and to give reasons for choices and observations.

Physical Development (PD)

By the end of the EYFS most children should:

PD1   Move with confidence, imagination and in safety.

PD2   Move with control and coordination.

PD3   Travel around, under, over and through balancing and climbing equipment.

PD4   Show awareness of space, of themselves and of others.

PD5   Recognise the importance of keeping healthy and those things which contribute to this.

PD6   Recognise the changes that happen to their bodies when they are active.

PD7   Use a range of small and large equipment

PD8   Handle tools, objects, construction and malleable materials safely and with increasing control.

Activities such as using clay, dough and construction toys will offer experience of PD8. Through pretending to decorate homes and clean windows children will have the opportunity to climb and move with control and imagination. Through using a range of small equipment as they play traditional garden games they will be encouraged to develop their coordination and control.

Throughout all the activities children are encouraged to talk about what they see and feel as they communicate their ideas in painting, collage work and role play.

Creative Development (C)

By the end of the EYFS most children should:

C1   Respond in a variety of ways to what they see, hear, smell, touch and feel.

C2   Express and communicate their ideas, thoughts and feelings by using a widening range of materials, suitable tools, imaginative and role-play, movement, designing and making, and a variety of songs and musical instruments.

C3   Explore colour, texture, shape, form and space in two or three dimensions.

C4   Recognise and explore how sounds can be changed, sing simple songs from memory, recognise repeated sounds and sound patterns and match movements to music.

C5   Use their imagination in art and design, music, dance, imaginative and role play and stories.

During this topic children will experience working with a variety of materials as they make models of homes, furniture and origami tulips. They will be able to develop their imaginations and skills of painting and colour mixing as they paint children who lived in a shoe and homes for nursery rhyme and fairy tale characters.

Week 1
My home

Personal, Social and Emotional Development

● Look at pictures of homes including flats, houses, caravans, castles, tents, boats and igloos. Talk about a home as a place where people feel comfortable and like to live. Encourage children to describe their own homes and to say why they like to live in them. (PS2, 5)

● Share the story of *Miss Brick the Builders' Baby* by Allan Ahlberg (Puffin). Talk about how it would feel for someone to break the model you have made. Discuss the need to handle other people's possessions sensitively and with care. (PS5, 9, 10)

Communication, Language and Literacy

● Help the children to complete the sentence 'My home is...' Write the sentences on strips of card and display them with the children's paintings of homes (See Creative Development section). (L11, 18, 19)

● Make a group big book of *The House that Jack Built* in the shape of a house. Encourage children to provide the illustrations and to write their own names for the cover. Look at features on a real book such as the author, illustrator, information on the back cover and bar code. As a group, ensure that all these features appear on your book. (L3, 4, 18)

● Start collecting words useful for a project on Houses and Homes. Encourage children to think of the initial and final sounds of the words, and to help with writing them. Display the words with the collection of pictures of different types of homes. (L5, 9, 18)

Problem Solving, Reasoning and Numeracy

● Use houses cut from card with doors numbered one to nine for number recognition and number ordering activities. (N1, 2, 3)

● Use the paintings of children's homes (see Creative Development) for data handling. Make a block graph to show the number of different coloured doors. Help children to find out which colour door is the most popular and the colours that are used the least. (N2, 9)

● Write the numbers from children's homes on house-shaped pieces of card. Use the houses for sorting. Ask questions such as: 'Which houses have a five in their number?' 'Do any houses have the same numbers?' Use numbers less than ten to arrange in numerical order. (N2, 3)

Knowledge and Understanding of the World

● Use the pictures of different types of homes. Encourage children to think about why they are suitable for particular people or places. Help children to be aware of the materials from which the homes are made. (K3)

● Make a model home (see activity opposite). (K5, 6)

● Use large wax crayons and paper to make rubbings of safe, outside walls. Encourage children to use magnifiers to observe the different patterns made. Ask parents/carers to help their child to do a rubbing at home and bring it in to add to a display. (K3)

Physical Development

● Encourage children to enjoy building homes with construction toys. (PD8)

● Put out a selection of large apparatus for children to enjoy climbing on. Encourage them to imagine the apparatus is a home and to enjoy visiting their friends. (PD1, 2, 7)

● Put out mats for children to use as role-play houseboats and benches as gangways and bridges. Tell a story in which children live in houseboats. Encourage them to think about the way the boats would rock on windy days and remind them to balance carefully on the benches so that they don't fall in the water! (PD1, 2, 3, 4)

Creative Development

● Use *So Many Babies* by Martina Selway (Hutchinson) as the stimulus for a group frieze of the old lady who lived in a shoe (see activity opposite). (CD3)

● Help children to paint pictures of their own homes. Encourage them to use accurate colours for doors, walls and so on. (CD3)

● Encourage children to enjoy playing in the role-play home corner. Over the next six weeks, change the items placed in it to give the feel of different types of home. Use boxes to mark out a boat-shaped home, stick large wheels on to create a caravan and use white paper marked with black brick lines to represent an igloo. (CD5)

Planning for Learning through Houses and homes

Practical Pre-School Books

Activity: Models of homes

Learning opportunity: Constructing homes using a range of materials.

Early Learning Goal: Knowledge and Understanding of the World. Children should build and construct with a wide range of objects, selecting appropriate resources and adapting their work where necessary. They should select the tools and techniques they need to shape, assemble and join the materials they are using.

Resources: Variety of boxes; cardboard tubes; corrugated card; scissors; PVA glue; masking tape; stiff card; ready-mixed paint; brushes; plastic trays; pencils, pictures of homes.

Key vocabulary: House, home, window, door, chimney, wall, roof, names for different types of homes and materials.

Organisation: Small group.

What to do: Show the children pictures of homes. Explain that they are going to make models of homes. Talk about the different types of homes that they might like to build. Invite children to look at the boxes and other materials and to select the items they feel would be useful.

Help children to construct the homes. Explain that they will be decorating the insides of their homes the following week and making furniture later on. Encourage children to take care to glue around edges of boxes and items to be stuck on and to count to ten several times whilst holding things together to stick firmly. If children want doors and windows cut out, ask them to draw the shapes before you do the cutting.

When the homes have been constructed, encourage children to paint the outsides of their models, taking care to leave no gaps.

Activity: Home in a shoe

Learning opportunity: Painting pictures of children.

Early Learning Goal: Creative Development. Children should explore colour, texture, shape (and) form... in two... dimensions.

Resources: A3-sized paper; paint; brushes; plastic paint pots; plastic mirrors; *So Many Babies* by Martina Selway

(Hutchinson); background showing a large shoe house on a large noticeboard.

Key vocabulary: House, shoe, children, many, names of colours.

Organisation: Whole group introduction, small group for painting activity.

What to do: Read *So Many Babies* by Martina Selway (Hutchinson). Encourage children to look closely at the illustrations and to think what a shoe would be like as a home. Show the group the shoe on the noticeboard. Explain that everyone is going to paint pictures of children to live in the shoe house.

Invite four children to come and paint. Look closely again at the pictures of children in the book and talk about who each child would like to paint. Some children may wish to base their painting on the book; others may prefer to paint themselves or a friend. As children paint, talk about the colours they are using. Ask them to paint the faces but leave the eyes and mouth for later when the paint has dried.

When finished, cut out the children, stick them onto black sugar paper and trim to give a thin black border. Invite children to choose where they would like their child to be placed on the frieze.

Display

Hang the numbered houses from a line with pegs. Nearby display the paintings of homes and block graph. Use words from the collection as labels for the paintings. Put out the model homes in a quiet area where children can enjoy going to view their work and the changes that take place over the project.

Week 2 Decorating

I like this wallpaper because...

Personal, Social and Emotional Development

● During a circle time, pass round wallpaper samples. Encourage children to take it in turn to complete sentences such as 'I like/do not like this wallpaper because...' and 'I would use this paper for ... because ...'. (PS2, 3, 5)

● Cut house-shaped pieces of wallpaper into jigsaw puzzles. Give pairs of children a jigsaw puzzle, a matching piece of house-shaped card, and glue. Encourage children to collaborate and take it in turn to place pieces of puzzle. Help children to stick the completed puzzles on to the sheets of card. (PS8)

Communication, Language and Literacy

● Tell children the story of how Milly-Molly-Mandy's family decorated her bedroom as a surprise ('Milly-Molly-Mandy has a surprise' in *More of Milly-Molly-Mandy* by Joyce Lankester Brisley (Puffin)). Encourage children to talk about how they would like their bedroom to be decorated. (L4)

● Make a role-play wallpaper shop. Put out paint colour charts, wallpaper samples and a range of crayons and pens for children to design their own papers. Encourage children to enjoy being the shop assistant who takes orders and writes bills and customers who describe the colours and patterns that they would like to buy. (L2, 7)

● Invite a painter and decorator to talk to the group about how to paint/wallpaper a room. Encourage children to listen carefully and to understand the variety of jobs that take place. Later make 'Thank you' cards for the visitor. (L3, 17)

Problem Solving, Reasoning and Numeracy

● Make a collection of paintbrushes ranging from thin ones suitable for painting pictures to big ones used to cover large walls. Encourage children to paint stripes and dots and to compare the sizes of marks they make (see activity opposite). (N11)

● Show children how to use regular, 3-d shapes and ready-mixed paint to print repeating patterns for wallpaper. (N10)

● From wallpaper stuck on card make 2-d shapes. Sort the shapes into sets according to the wallpaper patterns, the shape types and properties such as 'has/has not got three sides'. Encourage children to use the names for the shapes and to count the number in each set. (N1, 2, 11)

Knowledge and Understanding of the World

● Look at pictures to see how homes are decorated around the world. (K3)

● Investigate floor coverings such as cork tiles, carpet and lino. Encourage children to think about the properties a floor covering would need in a kitchen and a bedroom. Help children to compare the feel of the floor coverings and the ease with which a spilt cup of water can be cleared away. Talk about the games that children like to play in bedrooms and their preferred floors. Compare the way toy cars move over different floor surfaces. (K1, 3)

● Help children to decorate their model homes. Encourage them to give reasons for the choices that they make. Some children may wish to paint whilst others may prefer to use carpet samples, wallpaper, their own printed patterns and so on. (K5, 6)

Physical Development

● Put out a range of climbing and balancing equipment. Encourage children to pretend that they are decorating a house and to think about the rooms they are in as they balance across beams and climb ladders. At the finish encourage children to talk about the jobs they were doing and the colours of paint and patterns of wallpapers that they used. (PD1, 2, 3)

● Weave mats from brightly coloured strips of sugar paper (see activity opposite). (PD8)

Creative Development

● Show children a variety of paint charts. Talk about the way the paints next to each other often differ only slightly. Invite each child to pick a colour and then explore how many different tones they can make by adding white. Display the strips of colours as a gigantic paint chart. (C3)

● Provide each child with an A4-sized outline picture of a bedroom and crayons. Ask the children to decorate the walls and floor. When all the rooms have been completed help children to notice the way that colours can change rooms. (C1)

- Read *Old Bear's All-Together Painting* by Jane Hissey (Hutchinson). Encourage children to look closely at the patterns the toys made and the problems they had with paints that ran together and spots that turned into stripes. Invite children to paint patterns on A4 pieces of paper and later use the patterns to make a group picture. (C3)

Activity: Comparing brushes

Learning opportunity: Comparing sizes.

Early Learning Goal: Problem Solving, Reasoning and Numeracy. Children should use language such as 'circle' and 'bigger' to describe the shape and size of... flat shapes.

Resources: Variety of paint brushes including small ones for painting fine details and large ones for painting walls; paint; large pieces of paper.

Key vocabulary: Stripe, fat, thin, middle-sized, bigger, smaller.

Organisation: Small group.

What to do: Show the children the brushes. Together compare the heights and the quantity of bristles. Explain that it is important for painters to choose the right brushes when painting. Ask the group which brush they would use to paint a large wall and why. Then ask which would be good for doing a picture. Invite a child to paint a stripe with a medium-sized brush. Then invite another to choose a brush to paint a thicker stripe. Encourage children to take it in turn to paint stripes of varying thickness. Finally, as a group arrange the brushes in order for the thickness of stripes they paint.

Activity: Weaving mats

Learning opportunity: Weaving with thin card.

Early Learning Physical Development. Children will be able to handle tools (and) objects safely and with increasing control.

Resources: A5 card cut as a weaving frame; 15 x 3cm strips of colourful card; glue sticks; scissors; a finished mat.

Key vocabulary: Over, under, in, out, weave, mat, names of colours.

Organisation: Small group.

What to do: Show children the mat. Explain that it has been woven. Show children how to place glue on the end of a card strip, attach it to the top of the frame and weave. Encourage children to say 'under' and 'over' as the strips are woven and to anticipate where the strip is to go. Once children are happy with the idea of weaving, give each one a weaving frame and strips. Do not worry if the finished mats have missed gaps. Just help children to enjoy making them. When finished, glue any loose ends. Some children may like to use the mats in their model homes.

Display

Combine the wallpaper printing, the painted stripes, the wall rubbings and spare painted patterns to make a colourful group collage. Hang up the wallpaper shapes in a nearby draughty area. Place the bedroom colouring in clear plastic wallets and make a book of bedroom designs for the wallpaper shop. Involve children in suggesting suitable titles for the displays.

weaving frame

Trim end off card strip and glue.

Week 3
Furniture and household appliances

Personal, Social and Emotional Development

- Introduce the week's theme. Talk about the meanings of the words 'furniture' and 'household appliances'. Encourage children to say the words. Play 'I spy' using pictures and toy furniture and appliances. Involve children in giving clues that include colours, shapes, functions and places where the item might be found. (PS1, 3)

- Invite a parent who enjoys cooking to talk to the group about appliances that are useful to have in a kitchen. (PS1, 3)

Communication, Language and Literacy

- Provide catalogues and magazines for children to cut up and make catalogues of furniture for a particular room. Encourage children to write labels for the furniture and to use their catalogues for role play. (L2, 18)

- Provide each child with a folded sheet of white card to represent a fridge. Encourage children to fill their fridges with pictures of favourite foods and to write labels for the foods. (L18)

- As a group make an alphabet frieze of furniture and appliances. Encourage children to suggest items for each letter and to illustrate their ideas (see activity opposite). (L9, 10)

Problem Solving, Reasoning and Numeracy

- Use the story of 'Goldilocks and the Three Bears' as the stimulus for activities comparing sizes. Use props to tell the story inviting children to select the appropriate objects. As a group make up a new tale in which Goldilocks tries out a variety of appliances and furniture. Change the order so that the largest furniture/appliance is not always the first to be used. (N11)

- Play a game in which children are given instructions to place a toy under/on top/behind a chair or table. (N12)

- Involve children in making a record of the number of chairs, tables, beds, and so on, in a dolls' house. (N2, 3)

Knowledge and Understanding of the World

- Show children pictures of lights and people washing clothes before electricity was discovered. Encourage them to think about the benefits and disadvantages of electrical appliances. (K8)

- Investigate the stability of beds (see activity opposite). (K2)

- Provide safe rotary whisks for children to enjoy using in the water tray. Add bubble bath solution and encourage children to investigate how bubbles form as they whisk. (K1)

Physical Development

- Make decorations for fridge magnets from dough. When dry and painted, the decoration should be varnished by an adult. Ensure that it is completely dry before attempting to attach a magnet. (PD8)

- Provide construction toys for children to make furniture. Encourage children to talk about the things they make and to enjoy using them for role-play. (PD8)

Creative Development

- Help children to make furniture for the model homes. Encourage them to think about what they want to make before they select the materials they need. Show children how to cover plastic items with masking tape before painting them. (C2, 3)

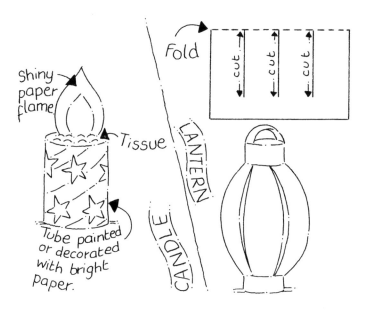

Fold

cut cut cut

Shiny paper flame

Tissue

Tube painted or decorated with bright paper.

LANTERN

CANDLE

- Remind children of the lights used in homes before electricity was discovered. Make lanterns and candles from cardboard tubes and brightly coloured paper. (C3)
- Show children how to undo the seams of cereal boxes and remake them inside out, with masking tape to provide a clean surface. Use the boxes and paints/felt pens for making televisions and radios. Use smaller boxes as telephones. Encourage children to enjoy using their telephones and to tell stories and sing songs for their radios and televisions. (C5).

Activity: Furniture frieze

Learning opportunity: Collaborating to make an alphabet frieze.

Early Learning Goal: Communication, Language and Literacy. Children should hear and say initial and final sounds in words. They will link sounds to letters, naming and sounding letters of the alphabet.

Resources: Large noticeboard covered with backing paper; lower case letters cut from sugar paper; A4 sized white paper; pencils; crayons; an alphabet frieze/poster; flip chart.

Key vocabulary: Furniture, appliance, names for furniture and appliances.

Organisation: Whole group.

What to do: Together look at the alphabet frieze/poster. Invite children to point out the initial sounds they recognise and to identify the corresponding pictures. Explain that you would like the group to have a frieze of furniture and appliances. Brainstorm names of pieces of furniture asking children to say the initial sound. Write

and draw their suggestions on a flip chart. Repeat this for appliances.

Invite children to draw their ideas on the A4 sized paper and to choose the letter cut from sugar paper that begins their word. Over the weeks, encourage children to add more pictures and appliances. Challenge them to find items for as many initial sounds as possible.

Activity: Investigating beds

Learning opportunity: Observing and comparing.

Early Learning Goal: Knowledge and Understanding of the World. Children should find out about and identify some features of... objects... they observe.

Resources: Teddy bear; A4 sized stiff card; four cardboard tubes (approx 10cm high); scissors; glue.

Key vocabulary: Bed, balance, numbers to four, corner, middle.

Organisation: Small group.

What to do: Explain that the teddy wants to buy a new bed. His old one broke and he wants to find out how many legs his bed needs for the bed to balance and give him a safe night's sleep.

Place one cardboard tube under the centre of the card. Ask children to predict what will happen when the bear lies on his bed. What would happen if he lay near the edge? Invite a child to place the bear on the bed. If it balances, ask children how safe the bear would be. Repeat the experiment with two, three and four tubes. Invite children to suggest where the tubes could be placed.

Finally, as a group make a bed from tubes and card for the teddy. If tubes are snipped and the pieces folded outwards they can be glued securely to the bed base.

Display

Display the pictures of furniture and appliances on a large noticeboard with the initial sounds cut from sugar paper. To encourage children to look closely at the display do not place all pictures for a given sound together. On a table in front put out an alphabet jigsaw and alphabet picture books. Label two hoops 'furniture that begins with b' and 'furniture that does not begin with b'. Put out the hoops with pictures/toy furniture for children to sort. Change the chosen letter each week.

Planning for Learning through Houses and homes

Week 4
Taking care of homes

Personal, Social and Emotional Development

- During a circle time make a list of all the people who help to take care of homes. Include people such as electricians, plumbers and window cleaners as well as family and friends. (PS3, 8)
- As a group talk about the things that children can do to help care for homes. (PS3, 8)
- Talk about the things that have to be done for special homes such as oiling wheels on mobile homes, checking that boats do not develop holes and cleaning windows on high-rise flats. (PS5)

Communication, Language and Literacy

- Enjoy sharing *An Evening At Alfie's* by Shirley Hughes. Talk about how Alfie might have felt when the leak started. Encourage children to act out the tale in the home corner. (L4, 7)
- As a group make a big book of ways to take care of a home. Include illustrations drawn by the children and captions suggested by them. Talk about the jobs that have to be done each day and those that are less frequent. Encourage children to think about the reasons for doing the jobs. (L3, 17)
- Make posters to encourage people to take care of their homes such as 'Wipe your feet!' (see activity opposite). (L17)

Problem Solving, Reasoning and Numeracy

- Make houseboats from foil. Float them in a water tray. Encourage children to count how many coins can be placed in the boats before they sink (see activity opposite). (N2)
- Remind children of the tidying and cleaning jobs that are done in homes. Talk about the importance of making good use of time. Invite children to see how many things they can do before the sand in a 20-second timer runs out. Challenges could include putting books on a shelf, polishing a table with a dry duster and sweeping up sand. (N6)
- Play a dice game in which the numbers represent jobs in a kitchen, such as 1 = floor cleaned, 2 = cups washed up and so on. The winner is the first child to clean their kitchen. (N1, 3)

Knowledge and Understanding of the World

- Provide pieces of scrap card and small watering cans for children to investigate the best shapes for house roofs on rainy days. Help children to realise why many homes have sloping roofs and why people often check their roofs before each winter comes. (K1, 2, 3)
- Invite children to place objects on a clean shelf. Each morning encourage children to check the shelf and to notice how long it takes for dust to form. (K3)
- Invite a parent to talk to the group about all the things they do to take care of a home. Encourage children to ask questions. (K4)

Physical Development

- Enjoy playing '(child's name) is in her/his home' to the tune of 'The farmer's in his den'. Encourage children to think of what each child might be doing at home and who they would like to call. This might include a window cleaner to wash windows, a plumber to mend a leak, a shopkeeper to deliver food and so on. Encourage children to be in role as they visit the home. (PD1, 2)
- Encourage children to think about machines that would be useful for looking after homes such as one that tidies bedrooms and hangs up clothes! Provide construction materials for children to enjoy inventing and making helpful machines for a home. (PD8)

Creative Development

- Help children to complete their model homes. Encourage them to check their models for loose pieces and areas where paint has been missed. Provide scraps of materials for making additional pieces of furniture, mats and decorations. (C3)

- Help children to make people for their homes by drawing, cutting out pictures from magazines or bending pipe-cleaners (see diagram below). (C3)

Activity: Helpful posters

Learning opportunity: Writing for a purpose.

Early Learning Goal: Communication, Language and Literacy. Children should attempt writing for various purposes, using features of different forms such as... instructions.

Resources: A4-sized paper; pencils; crayons.

Key vocabulary: Please, remember, poster, thank-you.

Organisation: Whole group.

What to do: Share the big book about ways to take care of a home. Talk about the things that are done each day and those that people might forget because they happen less frequently. Ask children to suggest jobs that are important such as remembering to lock doors at night and emptying rubbish bins before the refuse collection day. Tell the group that you would love to have some posters to remind you of the jobs you have to do at home. Explain that posters often have bright, clear pictures and a few words so that they are eye catching and easy to read from a distance. Invite children to suggest ideas for suitable posters.

Give each child a piece of A4 paper to draw a picture that explains the message of their poster. Finally, help them to overwrite/write a caption.

Activity: Foil houseboats

Learning opportunity: Counting and comparing.

Early Learning Goal: Problem Solving, Reasoning and Numeracy. Children should count reliably up to ten everyday objects.

Resources: Water tray; 1 pence coins; foil squares 10 x 10cm; picture of a house boat.

Key vocabulary: Float, sink, boat.

Organisation: Small group.

What to do: Together look at the picture of the houseboat. Talk about the need for people who live in houseboats to make good use of their space. Explain that some boats have beds that turn into seats during the day time. Also, talk about the importance of not overloading boats.

Give each child a piece of foil to press into a boat or bowl shape. Provide 1 pence coins for children to see how many their boats will hold and still float. If boats leak, press the joints firmly and talk about the importance of checking homes each year for possible needed repairs. Encourage children to enjoy comparing their designs and to investigate a variety of shapes.

Display

Put up the helpful posters around the room and, where possible, in places that are appropriate – one about emptying bins could be placed by the group's rubbish bin whilst one about cleaning windows would be near a window. Place the foil boats on a river made from blue material and edged with shells. Provide play people for children to enjoy using in the boats.

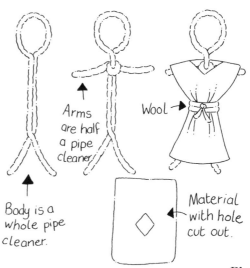

Week 5
In the garden

Personal, Social and Emotional Development

- Introduce the week's theme with a discussion about gardens. Ask children to describe gardens they have played in. Explain that not all homes have gardens. Talk about alternatives such as patios, courtyards, balconies, window boxes and hanging baskets. As a group plant out a large container with outdoor plants. (PS5)
- Talk about the 'Country Code'. As a group make a 'Garden Code' outlining how to behave safely in a garden. (PS9)

Communication, Language and Literacy

- Provide books made from folded A4-sized paper for children to make garden catalogues. Encourage children to include trees, flowers, play equipment and garden furniture and to label/write the initial sound for some items. (L18)
- Make a group alphabet book of flowers, minibeasts and made objects found in gardens. (L19)
- Read *Winnie in Winter* by Korky Paul and Valerie Thomas. Look closely at the pictures of Winnie's garden. Encourage children to talk about what they liked and disliked about the garden and to design new gardens for Winnie. (L4)

Problem Solving, Reasoning and Numeracy

- Use plastic plant pots of varying sizes and a sand tray to estimate and measure the capacities of a variety of containers. (N9)
- Use pictures of flowers cut from seed catalogues and greetings cards for sorting by colour. Encourage children to count how many pictures go in each colour set. Once sorted use the pictures to make a colourful garden collage with flowers arranged by colour. (N1, 2)
- Use the apple tree counting rhyme (see activity opposite). (N1, 2)

Knowledge and Understanding of the World

- Enjoy planting seeds and bulbs. Encourage children to take care of the things they plant and to describe the changes they notice as the plants grow. (K3)
- Talk about ponds and water features often found in gardens. Provide plastic bottles and funnels for children to investigate ways to make fountains and waterfalls. Help children to compare the way the water behaves when it is poured and when it is squeezed out of a plastic bottle. (K3)

Physical Development

- Use clay to make gnomes and animals for garden ornaments. (NB If children use hand cream before working with the clay hands are much easier to clean at the end!) (PD8)
- Play traditional outdoor games that children have enjoyed in gardens over the years. Provide hoops to roll and to jump in; soft balls to kick and throw and coloured bean bags for aiming into buckets. (PD7)
- Put out a range of outdoor toys for children to enjoy playing with imagination. (PD1, 7)

Creative Development

- Make origami tulips (see activity opposite). (C3)
- Use colourful papers, fabrics, sand, pasta, artificial/dried flowers and shells to make model gardens in shallow trays. (C3)
- Set out the role-play area as a garden centre. (C5)

Activity: Pick an apple

Learning opportunity: Enjoying counting with a number rhyme.

Early Learning Goal: Problem Solving, Reasoning and Numeracy. Children should say and use number names in order in familiar contexts. They should count reliably up to ten everyday objects.

Resources: *None required.*

Key vocabulary: Numbers to ten, apple, pip, grow, tree.

Organisation: Whole group sitting comfortably on the floor.

What to do: Recite the 'Pick an apple' rhyme below using your own name. Mime picking the apple, taking a large bite and picking out pips. Show five fingers to represent the pips. Repeat the rhyme with the group joining in. Invite a child to pick an apple. As a group say the rhyme and use the child's name. This time change the number of pips to two. Ask the group to show two fingers. At other times, choose different numbers of pips from one to ten.

(*Child's name*) picks an apple so juicy and round,
She/he bites the apple and counts the pips she's/he's found.
Five pips to plant and grow into trees,
With lots more apples for you and for me.

Activity: Origami tulip

Learning opportunity: Folding paper squares to make colourful flowers.

Early Learning Goal: Creative Development. Children should explore colour, shape, form and space in two or three dimensions.

Resources: Brightly coloured 15 x 15cm squares of paper; stalks and leaves cut from green sugar paper; a noticeboard with a garden background; real or pictures of tulips.

Key vocabulary: Fold, tulip, petals, flower, stalk, leaves.

Organisation: Small group.

What to do: Look at the tulips/pictures. Talk about the way many people like to have flowers around their homes. Explain that tulips can be made from paper (see diagram). Ask if anyone knows the name of the shape that is to be folded. Demonstrate and talk through each stage until all children have folded a flower.

Display

In preparation for the house-warming party, arrange the finished model homes with the gardens and gnomes in spaces around the room where they can be viewed but not knocked. Involve children in displaying their origami tulips on the noticeboard set out as a garden. Nearby place a basket of paper squares for children to make more folded flowers in spare moments.

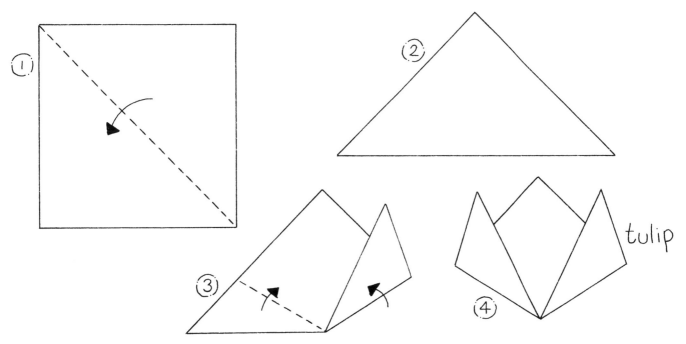

Week 6
Home for sale

Personal, Social and Emotional Development

- During a circle time talk about moving house. Encourage children to think about the things that they might miss and also the things they would like in a new home. (PS2, 3, 5)
- Talk about house-warming parties as times when people who have moved welcome friends to see their new home. Introduce the idea of the house-warming party that the group is going to host. (PS2, 3, 8)

Communication, Language and Literacy

- Look at examples of brochures describing homes from an estate agent. Make brochures for homes seen in picture books. Use them in role-play (See Creative Development section). (L11, 17)
- During a circle time encourage children to talk about the model homes they have made and to think about the things that make each one special. Help children to make 'For sale' posters for the model homes. (L8, 18)
- Help children to make invitations for the house-warming party. Encourage them to fill in the names of the people they would like to invite. (L18)

Problem Solving, Reasoning and Numeracy

- Use non-standard measures to help children find the sizes of their model homes (see activity opposite). (N2, 11)
- Show children four pictures of houses that vary slightly from each other in terms of the numbers of chimneys, doors and windows. Explain that the homes are for sale and give descriptions of the one you wish to buy. Encourage children to identify the home and to take it in turn to describe the ones they want to buy. (N1, 2)
- Repeat the above activity but with nine identical homes identifiable by numbers on their doors. Help children to identify the numbers one to nine and to arrange the homes in numerical order. (N3)

Knowledge and Understanding of the World

- Provide a range of construction toys for children to build homes for favourite fairy tale and nursery rhyme characters. Encourage children to think about the features that would help to make their home ideal for the chosen character. (K5)
- Invite an estate agent or parent that has recently moved house to talk to the group about selling and buying homes. (K8)
- Investigate the best materials for writing 'For sale' signs. Encourage children to realise that the signs need to be waterproof. Help them to compare the effect of pouring water over notices written in paint, felt pen, wax crayon and pencil. (K2, 3, 4)

Physical Development

- Play 'Home for sale' (see activity opposite). (PD3)
- Encourage children to enjoy using climbing equipment as they pretend to get homes ready to sell. (PD7)

Creative Development

- Provide modelling dough and scrap materials for children to enjoy making house-warming presents, such as thumb pots, for their friends. (C3)
- Set up the role-play area as an estate agent's. Encourage children to enjoy being both customers and agents. Provide a dolls' house for children to enjoy taking dolls on guided tours of the potential new home. (C5)
- Paint pictures of suitable homes for fairy tale and nursery rhyme characters. (C3)

Activity: Measuring homes

Learning opportunity: Using non-standard measures and counting.

Early Learning Goal: Problem Solving, Reasoning and Numeracy. Children should count reliably up to ten

18

Planning
for Learning
through
Houses and
homes

Practical Pre-School Books

everyday objects. They should use language such as 'bigger' to describe the size of solids and flat shapes.

Resources: Model homes; non-standard measures, for example toy bricks, books, cotton reels, playing cards, pencils; A3 paper; pencils; crayons.

Key vocabulary: How long?, measure, numbers to ten, width, length.

Organisation: Whole group introduction, pairs for the measuring activity.

What to do: Tell children the traditional tale of a king who wanted a new bed. He measured the size of the bed in paces and passed the measurements on to a carpenter. Sadly the carpenter had smaller feet and the bed was too small.

Explain that today they are going to measure their homes. As a group decide what will be used to measure the heights of the houses. Suitable measures might include toy bricks, books, cotton reels, playing cards and pencils. Help children to measure the heights and record them on folded pieces of A3 paper. Repeat the activity for the widths and lengths. Encourage children to think about when it would be useful to know the sizes of homes. Help them to compare the sizes of the homes. Finally, invite children to decorate their pieces of folded paper like details for a home in an estate agent's.

~~~~~~

Activity: Home for sale

Learning opportunity: Moving to a traditional skipping rhyme.

Early Learning Goal: Physical Development. Children should move with control and coordination.

Resources: Plastic hoop.

Key vocabulary: Words in the rhyme, skip.

Organisation: Whole group.

What to do: Teach the group the traditional skipping rhyme:

Home for sale
Apply within,
When (*child's name*) goes out
(*New child's name*) can come in.

Explain any unfamiliar words. Show the group the hoop and explain that it is the home. Invite a child to stand in the home. Form a circle around the hoop with the rest of the group. Holding hands skip around the hoop and sing the song using the tune for the first two lines of 'Twinkle, twinkle, little star'. In the final line the child at the centre suggests the name of the next person to live in the home. She or he joins the circle and the new child skips into the hoop.

Display

Near the role-play estate agent's put up a sign saying 'Homes for sale!'. Display the posters and the leaflets about the model homes. Nearby put up the paintings of homes for fairy tale and nursery rhyme characters. In a book box put out nursery rhyme and fairy tale books. Involve children in checking they are happy with the way that their model homes are set out and place a 'sold' sign on each one.

Planning
for Learning
through
Houses and homes

Bringing It All Together

A house-warming party provides a valuable opportunity for children to enjoy showing family and friends activities and displays from the Houses and Homes project.

Timing

The ideal time to host the house-warming party is outside of the normal times when the group meets. Then, children can show their family and friends their model home in a calm way, taking as much time as they need. The event could be held during a group meeting time, but all the children and adults would be present at the same time, resulting in a less relaxed occasion.

Preparation

Remind children that house-warming parties allow people who have new homes to show them to their friends and families and to celebrate together. Explain that the children will have to send out invitations, tidy their homes and prepare food and drinks. During the party they will be able to give tours of their homes and look after their visitors. They will be able to share favourite activities and displays from the Houses and Homes topic.

Tell children that visitors sometimes send 'Welcome to your new home' cards and even bring presents. Within folded pieces of A4 card write each child's name. Share the cards out so that each child makes a 'Welcome to your home' card for another. Provide plain paper for children to decorate with felt pen or wax crayon patterns. Help children to use the paper to wrap up the house-warming presents made from modelling dough and scrap materials.

Encourage the children to practise giving tours of their homes to friends. Also, through questions, reinforce earlier activities and displays that they may wish to share

Food

Involve children in making a fruit punch from fruit juices, lemonade and pieces of fruit. Make house and people-shaped biscuits. Ask for contributions of finger food from parents and involve children in making thank-you cards for any offerings.

The house-warming party

Encourage children to show their model homes to their families and friends and try out activities used during the topic. Help children to pour the fruit punch into plastic beakers, to carry it and to offer refreshments. Finally, when children and their visitors are ready to leave give them their house-warming presents and cards.

Resources

Resources to collect
- Flower, furniture and appliances catalogues.
- Safe rotary whisks.
- Samples of wallpaper, floor coverings and curtains.
- Paint charts.
- Cash register and receipt pad.

Everyday resources
- Large and small boxes for modelling.
- Papers and cards of different weights, colours and textures, for example sugar, corrugated card, silver and shiny papers and so on.
- Dry powder paints for mixing and mixed paints.
- Different-sized paint brushes from household brushes to thin brushes for delicate work and a variety of paint mixing containers.
- A variety of drawing and colouring pencils, crayons, pastels and so on.
- Additional decorative and finishing materials such as sequins, foils, glitter, tinsel, shiny wool and threads, beads, pieces of textiles, parcel ribbon.
- Table covers.
- Pasta.
- Clay.

Stories
- *Miss Brick the Builder's Baby* by Allan Ahlberg (Puffin).
- *Old Bear's All-Together Painting* by Jane Hissey (Hutchinson).
- *An Evening at Alfie's* by Shirley Hughes (Red Fox).
- *More of Milly-Molly-Mandy* by Joyce Lankester Brisley (Puffin).
- *Winnie in Winter* by Korky Paul and Valerie Thomas (Oxford University Press).
- *So Many Babies* by Martina Selway (Red Fox).
- Fairy tales from the Ladybird *Favourite Tales* collection:
    Goldilocks and the Three Bears
    Little Red Riding Hood
    Hansel and Gretel
    The Enormous Turnip
- Look in libraries for *Oh No, Peedie Peebles!* by Mairi Hedderwick (Red Fox) which is currently out of print. This story tells of a family trying to decorate a house whilst their toddler, Peedie Peebles, makes a lot of mess with paints!

Songs
- *Okki-tokki-unga Action Songs for Children* chosen by Beatrice Harrop, Linda Friend and David Gadsby (A & C Black Ltd).

Poems
- *This Little Puffin: Finger Plays and Nursery Rhymes* by Elizabeth Matterson (Puffin).

Resources for planning
- *The Early Years Foundation Stage: Setting the Standards for Learning, Development and Care for Children from Birth to Five* (Department for Children, Schools and Families.)

Collecting Evidence of Children's Learning

Monitoring children's development is an important task. Keeping a record of children's achievements, interests and learning styles will help you to see progress and will draw attention to those who are having difficulties for some reason. If a child needs additional professional help, such as speech therapy, your records will provide valuable evidence.

Records should cover all the areas of learning and be the result of collaboration between group leaders, parents and carers. Parents should be made aware of your record keeping policies when their child joins your group. Show them the type of records you are keeping and make sure they understand that they have an opportunity to contribute. As a general rule, your records should form an open document. Any parent should have access to records relating to his or her child. Take regular opportunities to talk to parents about children's progress. If you have formal discussions regarding children about whom you have particular concerns, a dated record of the main points should be kept.

Keeping it manageable

Records should be helpful in informing group leaders, adult helpers and parents and always be for the benefit of the child. The golden rule is to make them simple, manageable and useful.

Observations will basically fall into three categories:
- **Spontaneous records:** Sometimes you will want to make a note of observations as they happen, for example, a child is heard counting cars accurately during a play activity, or is seen to play collaboratively for the first time.

- **Planned observations:** Sometimes you will plan to make observations of children's developing skills in their everyday activities. Using the learning opportunity identified for an activity will help you to make appropriate judgements about children's capabilities and to record them systematically.

To collect information:
- talk to children about their activities and listen to their responses;
- listen to children talking to each other;
- observe children's work such as early writing, drawings, paintings and 3D models. (Keeping photocopies or photographs is useful.)

Sometimes you may wish to set up 'one off' activities for the purposes of monitoring development. Some pre-school groups, for example, ask children to make a drawing of themselves at the beginning of each term to record their progressing skills in both co-ordination and observation. Do not attempt to make records after every activity!

- **Reflective observations:** It is useful to spend regular time reflecting on the children's progress. Aim to make some brief comments about each child every week.

Informing your planning

Collecting evidence about children's progress is time consuming and it is important that it is useful. When you are planning, use the information you have collected to help you to decide what learning opportunities you need to provide next for children. For example, a child who has poor pencil or brush control will benefit from more play with dough or construction toys to build the strength of hand muscles.

Example of recording chart

Name: Leanne Field		D.O.B. 31.1.04			Date of entry: 13.11.08	
Term	**Personal, Social and Emotional Development**	**Communication, Language and Literacy**	**Problem Solving, Reasoning and Numeracy**	**Knowledge and Understanding of the World**	**Physical Development**	**Creative Development**
ONE	Happy to say goodbye to mother. Enjoys collaborative play. 23.9.08 CT	Enjoys listening to stories. Particularly enjoys reciting rhymes. Can write first and last names. Often reverses 'e'. Good pencil grip 2.10.08 RES	Is able to say numbers to ten and count accurately five objects. Enjoyed the bedtime rhyme. Recognises and names squares. 15.10.08 EHL	Very eager to ask questions. Enjoyed investigating papers for books. Good scissor control. 29.9.08 JT	Very flexible. Can balance on one leg. Loved trying to juggle.Does not like the feel of playdough. 7.11.08 SJS	Made a wonderful bookmark. Loves scissors and glue! Enjoys mixing own colours. 30.10.08 CCM
TWO						
THREE						

Skills overview of six-week plan

Week	Topic Focus	Personal, Social and Emotional Development	Communication, Language and Literacy	Problem Solving, Reasoning and Numeracy	Knowledge and Understanding of the World	Physical Development	Creative Development
1	My home	Listening; Expressing emotions; Sensitivity to others' feelings	Listening and responding to stories; Writing; Recognising initial and final sounds	Recognising numbers; Counting; Sorting; Comparing	Making observations; Comparing; Constructing	Moving with control and imagination; Using construction tools; Climbing and balancing	Role-play; Painting
2	Decorating	Listening; Taking turns; Sensitivity to others' needs	Listening; Responding to stories; Writing; Role-play	Counting; Comparing 2-D shapes; Recognition of shapes; Ordering size	Comparing; Describing; Investigating; Painting, cutting and sticking	Moving with control, safety and imagination; Climbing; Balancing; Weaving	Painting; Colouring; Collage
3	Furniture and appliances	Showing interest; Concentrating and sitting quietly	Writing labels; Role-play; Linking sounds to letters; Recognising initial and final sounds	Comparing sizes; Counting; Understanding positional language	Talking; Investigating; Observing; Finding out about domestic chores in the past	Using malleable and construction materials	Singing; Painting; Colouring with caroyns; Constructing; Role-play
4	Taking care of homes	Maintaining attention and sitting quietly; Being aware of others' needs	Responding to a story; Role-play; Writing for a purpose	Counting; Recognising numbers; Comparing	Talking; Observing; Comparing; Investigating; Asking questions	Moving with control and imagination; Using construction materials	Using materials; Cutting; Constructing
5	In the garden	Listening; Speaking; Being aware of others' needs; Understanding what is right and wrong	Responding to a story; Recognising initial sounds; Discussing and writing captions	Counting; Estimating and comparing; Comparitive language	Investigating; Observing; Talking	Using small and large equipment; Aiming; Using malleable materials	Collage; Making model gardens; Role-play
6	Home for sale	Expressing emotions; Maintaing attention; Collaborative planning	Listening to a story; Writing for a purpose; Talking to clarify feelings	Recognising numbers; Counting; Using non-standard measures	Observing; Investigating; Comparing; Asking questions; Talking; Constructing	Moving with imagination, control and coordination; Climbing	Using materials; Role-play; Painting

Home links

The theme of Houses and Homes lends itself to useful links with children's homes and families. Through working together children and adults gain respect for each other and build comfortable and confident relationships.

Establishing partnerships

● Keep parents informed about the topic of Houses and Homes and the themes for each week. By understanding the work of the group, parents will enjoy the involvement of contributing ideas, time and resources.
● Photocopy the parent's page for each child to take home.
● Invite friends, childminders and families to share in the house-warming party.

Visiting enthusiasts

● Invite adults to come to the group to talk about decorating, moving house and jobs done to take care of homes.

Resource requests

● Ask parents to contribute left-over wallpaper, carpet, cork tiles, curtain fabric and other materials that could be used to decorate model homes. Ask them to collect boxes, cardboard tubes and any other materials suitable for constructing homes, furniture and gardens.
● Catalogues, greetings cards and colour magazines are invaluable for collage work and a wide range of interesting activities.

The house-warming party

● It is always useful to have extra adults at times such as the house-warming party.
● Ask parents to contribute finger foods.
● Invite a parent with a digital camera to take photos of all the model homes. Use the photos to make a book about the house-warming party.